Scavengers and Decomposers:
The Cleanup Crew

Contents

Scavengers and Decomposers:
The Cleanup Crew

1.

The Cleanup Crew

ABOVE THE PLAINS OF AFRICA a soaring vulture spots a dead wildebeest. He glides down and lands clumsily on top of it. His strong hooked beak tears at the flesh. Within minutes, more of the large brown birds alight. Vultures surround and nearly cover the carcass as their naked red heads grab for the meat.

A lioness roars and pounces on the carcass. The vultures flap a few feet away. They stand watching, as the lioness gulps great mouthfuls. One vulture walks slowly toward the food. He is nearly within reach. The lioness growls and swings her sharp-clawed paw at him. He jumps back, flapping his wings. Suddenly he lunges forward, snatches a piece of meat and flies out of reach. Other vultures sneak forward and grab bites, while the lioness eats.

Growls, yells, and a shriek like loud laughter startle the birds as six hyenas rush across the dry grass. The doglike animals gather behind the lioness.

One jumps forward and nips at her hind leg. Quickly he leaps back as she whirls to attack. Another jumps in, snaps, and dashes to safety. She swings at him. The hyenas trot back and forth, keeping to the lioness's rear and taking turns jumping in to bite. Finally she gives up and lopes away.

The hyenas crowd around the feast, eating as fast as they can. They push and shove and fill the air with laughter and yells. Their feast lasts only a few moments. Their laughter is stilled by one hyena's alarm cry.

Two male lions stride into view. The hyenas scatter. For hours they lie in a circle watching the lions, as the two beasts eat their fill. The vultures, too, watch as their meal disappears.

After the lions leave, the hyenas take over again. When they finish, there is nothing left. The vultures must take to the skies again to search for another meal.

Vultures live in many countries besides Africa. You can see them soaring overhead when you travel in a car along a highway. Their wings outstretched and motionless, they ride the air currents with the grace and beauty of hang gliders. Farther down the road, a car may startle some of the big birds tearing at the flesh of a dead rabbit. On the ground they plod clumsily around their food.

Vultures like these, and thousands of other

scavengers, help keep the world clean and beautiful. They are part of nature's cleanup crew. The other half of this recycling team are the decomposers (living organisms that break down wastes and dead material into simple compounds). Bacteria and fungi are decomposers. For example: Mushrooms that pop up in lawns are the fruit part of one kind of

fungus decomposer. The rest of the plant is underground digesting dead grass and turning it into food living grasses can use. Without this team of scavengers and decomposers there could be no life on earth.

Every day tons of once-living material fall to the ground. Animals and plants die. Leaves, flowers, hair and skin fall from plants and animals. Dung is dropped by all animals. Life on earth would be buried under this mass of dead material if something did not remove it. If the chemicals in it were not returned to the soil and air, there would be no food for plants or animals. Life would disappear from the earth.

All the chemicals needed for living things to

exist are limited to those already on or near the surface of the earth and dissolved in its waters. There is only a certain amount of each of these chemical elements. These elements must be used over and over again to keep life going. Chemicals that were in your sandwich at lunch may have been in the grass munched by a brontorsaurus millions of years ago. All the years in between they have been used over and over by other plants and animals. Plants turn the chemicals into food for animals. Some animals eat plants. Other animals eat them.

Gardeners and farmers bury manure (dung used for fertilizer) in the ground to provide food for the plants they grow. In the wild, animals drop their dung on the ground. This dung is loaded with the chemicals plants need. But plants cannot use these chemicals in this form because their roots can't absorb them. They must be changed to different chemical combinations. Decomposers make these changes.

For example, plants need nitrogen to grow. Much of the nitrogen in manure is combined with other chemicals in complex forms. Plants cannot absorb these particles. Bacteria in the soil break them down into simpler particles the plants can use.

Let's follow a nitrogen atom through one possible cycle. A mouse eats a bean. Some of the nitrogen in the bean is used to build his muscles. The

owl eats the mouse and uses some of the nitrogen to build his body. After he dies, the vulture finds and eats him. He uses some of the nitrogen in the owl's body for his own body. Some of it he deposits as dung. In just a few days decomposers change the nitrogen in the dung into forms plants can use. If decomposers had to work on the owl's body without a scavenger's help, it would take many weeks.

Scavengers of all sizes digest dead plants and animals for their own needs and produce dung. The decomposers dissolve the dung and change it to food for themselves and nutrients plants can use. Scavengers are everywhere. They work in the air, the water and the soil. Some are small insects or worms. Others are fish or land animals. Wherever they are, scavengers and decomposers are nature's cleanup crew, ridding the earth of organic garbage and providing food for all living things.

2.

Bird Scavengers

TURKEY AND BLACK VULTURES (often called buzzards in the United States) are full-time scavengers. Their talons are too dull and straight and their feet too clumsy and weak to often catch living animals. Occasionally they will catch a small animal such as a snake or mouse that they happen to blunder into, but they do not hunt living prey. Their hunt is a search for the already dead.

There are not as many carcasses as there are living animals. Vultures must search for each meal, and they are well-adapted for this search. Their wings are broad and long. Without a wingbeat they can soar for hours, riding the air currents. In this way they search many square miles without using much energy.

With long-range eyesight far keener than man's, they can spot a dead animal from a mile or more above the treetops. When one vultures dives, others soaring within a few miles spot it and follow. More of the big birds see these followers and come to join the feast. When a vulture finds a meal, it usually has to share it.

A hungry turkey vulture may have to wait if it finds a freshly killed animal. Its beak and claws are too weak to tear through the skin and tough flesh of some carcasses. It must wait for the flesh to soften. Patiently it stands by, testing the carcass every so often with its blunt curved beak, like a cook stabbing dinner on the stove to see if it is done. If it is a hot day, or the sun is shining on the carcass, the heat will help soften the meat.

The turkey vulture lives in Canada and the United States. This bird's brownish-black body is over two feet long. Its wings open to span six feet. A featherless head and neck with red and wrinkled skin protrudes from its bulky body. The black vulture lives in the southern states and south through Central America. Its brownish-black neck is also naked and wrinkled. Its body is even larger than the turkey vulture's.

Both these birds have a difficult time getting their heavy bodies into the air. They run and flap their long wings frantically until they finally stagger upward. Sometimes they eat so much they cannot take off at all. They have to stay on the ground until they digest part of their meal and lighten their load by dropping some dung.

Vultures may be clumsy on the ground, but they are creatures of grace and beauty in the air. Maybe you have lain in the sun-warmed grass of summer and watched them soar. With motionless wings outstretched, they spiral upward and circle over the woods nearby. Occasionally one glides silently down to treetop level, then spirals upward again, so high it is a tiny mark among the white clouds. You might imagine you're soaring with them. Higher and higher you float on a soft breeze-cushion.

Suddenly something blacks out the sun. You jump up in fright to find a vulture flying above you. You have been lying so quietly during your flying dream, the bird thought you might be dead. It almost landed on you to check you out for its next meal.

There are nine different species of vultures on the American continent and many more in Europe, Asia, and Africa. Old World vultures have claws and beaks more like hunting birds. Their beaks are stronger and sharper, their legs and toes shorter and more powerful, and their claws sharper and curved for clutching. They catch live prey as well as eating already dead animals.

The California condor, the largest bird in North America, is also a vulture. This bird weighs twenty to twenty-five pounds. Its wings open to span up to eleven feet. For many years ranchers put poison in sheep carcasses to kill coyotes and wolves. The condors ate from these poisoned carcasses and from the bodies of the wolves and coyotes who were poisoned. Many of them were killed and now the bird is almost extinct. The few that remain live in the mountains of southern California.

Many vultures have learned to patrol roads and highways, looking for small animals killed by automobiles. On roads and in the streets of some towns they are a part of a regular street cleaning operation. When you travel by bus or automobile, watch for vultures feeding or clumsily taking off beside the road.

If you are lucky enough to be in or near the country, perhaps you can lie in the grass and watch them soar. If you do, wave to them once in a while to let them know you are alive.

There are many smaller bird scavengers, too. Every year ravens, crows, and jays remove thousands of pounds of carrion from our highways. They also feed on dead fish and other carrion along the shores of streams and lakes. Black crows and ravens gather with the larger vultures and eagles along some of the rivers in western United States to feed on dead and dying fish during the annual salmon runs. Sometimes so many birds line up along the river banks that they almost rub shoulders.

Sea gulls form another large part of our flying cleanup crew. Millions of gulls range over most of the world from the arctic cold to the tropics. These sturdy, short-tailed birds soar on long, pointed wings. They come in all sizes from that of a small robin (eight to ten inches long) to a large duck size (about two feet). Black, brown, and white patterns give each species its special look. Most gulls live along seacoasts. Some travel far inland and others out to sea. You may see flocks of them standing on their small webbed feet or soaring overhead along beaches or around garbage dumps. Since they will eat almost anything, they pick up garbage wherever they go.

Gulls at sea eat dead fish, refuse of all kinds, and fish that swim near the surface. In ports they gather around boats and ships, waiting for garbage that is thrown over the side. Other fish-eating birds, such as pelicans, also follow fishing boats, eating the fish wastes thrown overboard.

At the seashore it is fun to throw bread into the air for beach-patrolling gulls to catch. When they are not getting a free handout, they clean up carrion and garbage left on the sand. Imagine what a smelly mess a beach could be after a storm has washed in lots of dead sea life, if it were not cleaned up.

After a storm, birds from inland sometimes come and help the gulls. Sea gulls, crows, ravens and vultures also consume tons of animal and plant matter from open garbage dumps. They are often joined there for dinner by scavenging animals.

3.

Mammals

BEARS AND BIRDS eat together along rivers during salmon season. The salmon die after swimming upstream and laying their eggs. Bears catch them alive and scavenge for them after they die. It is all the same to the bears. Salmon are food, dead or alive. So many bears gather at some of the fishing spots that the younger ones are crowded out. Sometimes the only fish these smaller bears get are the dead ones left after the bigger bears have eaten their fill.

In the spring, scavenging provides the grizzly bear with a big share of its food. Winter's cold and food shortages kill the weaker deer, antelope, moose and elk. Their bodies provide a feast for the hungry grizzly when it emerges from hibernation.

Grizzlies and ravens sometimes cooperate in their scavenging. The skin of a big animal is too tough for even the raven's stout bill to tear through. But it can fly, and so it finds dead bodies more easily than the bear. A grizzly will follow the circling ravens to find a carcass. Its strong jaws and sharp teeth open up the meat. The ravens can then join their huge companions for a feast.

Raccoons and some bears eat almost anything. They scavenge along shores, in the forests, and in garbage cans and dumps. Alaskan brown bears are particularly fond of the rotting bodies of seals, walruses, and whales that wash ashore. In some of our national parks bears and raccoons appear every night to eat their fill in garbage dumps. Campers who neglect to seal their food in animal-proof containers may lose it to raiding bears or raccoons. Raccoons even venture into towns to dump garbage cans, especially those that smell of fish or chicken.

As the darkness falls on a city and people begin going to sleep, another population is just waking up. Rats and mice come scurrying out. Along the buildings and from shadow to shadow they dash in search of food. They paw through trash piles and garbage cans. Water does not stop them. They swim out in the rivers to gather garbage that floats there. There are many more rats and mice in the world than there are people. They live everywhere: in cities and towns, on ships, in fields, barns, forests, deserts, and along lakes and streams. Some eat only meat, others plants. Many eat both. Nearly all rats and mice scavenge at least part of the time. In houses mice eat food wherever they find it. They clean up crumbs on the floor and shelves and eat garbage in open containers. Unfortunately, they also eat food we have stored in containers they can chew through. Outside, rats and mice scavenge food left in fields and orchards after the harvest, plant materials that grew wild, garbage dumped out in open, and dead insects and small animals. Some rats and mice are also hunters.

The big brown Norway rat with his long and scaly tail and the little light-brown house mouse are natives of Europe and Asia. They invaded America by stowing away on ships. The house mouse traveled with the Pilgrims. Both of these rodents eat any kind of food and some things you might not think of as food, such as motor oil, glue, soap, and candles. Like many scavengers, Norway rats also hunt. They eat lizards, insects and other small animals that come their way.

Stories have been told for many years about the brave lions and cowardly hyenas. We may think of lions as bold hunters and hyenas as sneaky critters who slink around waiting for the lions' leftovers.

Actually the story is much different. Both lions and hyenas are hunters. But it is not easy to catch your dinner when it runs faster than you can. A hunter usually chases several animals before it manages to catch one. For hungry lions and hyenas any meat is a meal. If it is already dead, so much the better; it can't run away. Lions and hyenas both scavenge when they get the chance.

Hyenas usually hunt in packs. When these dog-like animals kill their prey or find some carrion, they are a noisy bunch. They growl, yelp, and howl their hyena laughter. Lions hearing all this racket know the hyenas have something to eat. Two or three lions often chase off a pack of hyenas and steal their food. Twitching their short, tasselled tails, the hyenas wait impatiently for the lions to finish. The big cats always leave something for the smaller animals, even if it is only bones and pieces of skin. Hyenas are efficient scavengers because their jaws and teeth are so strong they can crush the biggest bones and chew the toughest hides.

Because they are such good scavengers, some African villages invite hyenas to stop by and pick up the garbage every night. An opening is left in

the wall around the village. The garbage is put outside the huts. Hyenas come and clean it up. Remembering that hyenas are also hunters, people make sure their children are inside after dark. Some villages even have a hyena man, who hand-feeds scraps to the hyenas to encourage their return.

Jackals, a kind of African wild dog, sometimes scavenge alongside hyenas. They grab at the food quickly to avoid the hyena's strong teeth. With their long noses, pointed ears and bushy tails, jackals look like long-legged foxes. They eat fruit, insects, snakes, and meat from animals they kill, as well as carrion and garbage. Like hyenas, they scavenge around villages and hunt in packs for larger animals. They often vie with hyenas and vultures to get what lions, leopards and tigers leave.

All meat-eating mammals that scavenge are also hunters. In hunting or scavenging their search is simply for something to eat. While satisfying their need for food by scavenging, they also speed up nature's recycling.

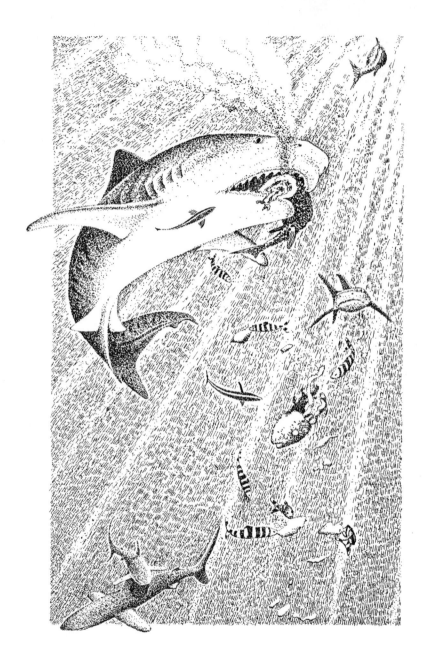

4.

Ocean
and Fresh Water
Scavengers

COMPETITION FOR FOOD in the water is much the same as it is on land. Herbivores eat plants and carnivores eat meat. Scavengers consume dead plant and animal material. Water animals depend on green plants for food just as land animals do. Ocean-growing plants must live near enough to the surface to get the sunlight they need for life. Where there is no sunlight, there are no green plants.

Below six hundred feet the ocean is dark. Green plants do not grow there. Therefore, there are fewer animals and less food than above. All life in these depths depends on what falls from above. Scavengers live at all depths, from the surface to the ocean floor.

Near the surface, plants grow and are eaten. Small fish and other animals are eaten by larger carnivores. Scavengers clean up dead animal and plant material they find.

Sharks are one of the best known carnivores of the ocean. They are messy eaters. As they tear chunks from their prey, small pieces drift off into the water. While sharks grab and gulp, remoras and pilotfish carefully pick up scraps from their dinners. Pilotfish and remoras are constant companions of tropical sharks, joining them for dinner each time they eat.

The light and dark blue-striped pilotfish swim just below and behind the heads of sharks. They were named pilotfish, because people thought they led sharks to food. Actually they follow the sharks, waiting for a free meal.

Remoras get a free ride as well as a free meal. With oval suction discs on top of their heads they fasten themselves to sharks and ride along until food appears. After the meal is over they attach to the nearest sharks and ride around waiting for the next meal.

Small pieces missed by the remoras and pilotfish drift with the ocean's currents like seeds in the wind. They are picked up by other scavengers as they gradually sink toward the bottom. A constant rain of dead and dying plants and animals drifts down. All the way down, scavengers devour the bodies and pieces of debris.

By the time this rain reaches the dark depths, much of it has been consumed. Little falls as far as the bottom in the deep seas. What does is in very small pieces. It lands on a layer of sediment often several feet deep. Even on the floor in these dark depths scavengers search for food in the debris.

Green plants cannot live there, for no sunlight reaches that deep. The only members of the plant kingdom to be found are bacteria and fungi. These tiny plants include the bacteria that cause decay and fungi similar to molds and mildews we find in damp places on land. They do not have chlorophyll or roots, so they cannot make their own food as green plants do. They feed on dead material that gathers in the sediment. As on land, they change this dead material into simpler chemical compounds. Ocean currents carry these compounds back to the upper layers, where green plants can use them.

Without scavengers and decomposers, materials that rain down would remain deposited on the ocean bottom, and they would not return to again be avail-

able to the plants above. Life in the oceans would end.

Nutrients for life on land would be lost, too. Carried to the oceans by rivers and dumped by people as garbage and in sewage plant discharge, these nutrients join the oceans' rain of debris. Man and animals return nutrients to the land by using plants and animals from the sea for food and fertilizer.

Tons of fish and other seafood are taken from the seas by fishermen around the world every year. We eat it and feed it to our pets. Parts not used for food are made into fertilizer for plants.

Dead sea plants and animals wash ashore on the beaches. Here scavengers find them. Besides the sea gulls you may have watched at the beach, there are many small beach scavengers.

Have you seen little crabs scurrying about on the beach and popping into holes to hide when they spotted you? They feed on small particles brought in on the waves.

If you pick up seaweed on the beach, you may see animals with long antennas hopping about like small grasshoppers. Beach hoppers and sand fleas keep cool and damp there while they eat decaying seaweed and other plant debris brought in by the ocean.

On a rocky shore you can find a great number of different animals. Many of them are scavengers.

Often there are thousands of mussels fastened to a single rock face. Between these large clamlike animals you can see barnacles, tiny shrimp, worms, snails and other small creatures. As tides rise to cover the rocks, and waves splash over them, these animals harvest their food from the water.

VARIETIES OF these animals can also be found in fresh water. If you explore a small lake or pond with plants and animals in it, you also can find scavengers. Some live on or just under the surface of the water. These surface dwellers eat dead and dying plants and animals that fall in or float to the top.

Swimming about in the water or climbing around on rocks and plants you may see insects, snails, and fish.

The bottom of the pond is especially rich with scavengers. Snails, insects, worms, clams, and crustacea, such as crayfish, may live there. Some of these bottom dwellers burrow into the mud and rest during the day. Some also swim through the water and may even crawl out on rocks and plants.

Pond scavengers come in many sizes from one-celled animals to fishes, crayfish and clams. Look and see what you can find in a pond you can visit.

Can you see some insects walking, hopping or swimming on the surface? Most of them can stay on top because their bodies are very light. Some have waxy hairs that repel water. A water strider has these hairs on its feet. The hairs make it possible for the strider to be supported on the surface film, as it walks on its jointed stilt-like legs.

Did you see a brown beetle speeding around in circles on the surface? It is a whirligig beetle. The hard shell over its lightweight body is smooth and streamlined. Two pairs of broad, fringed legs work like paddles. It kicks them so fast they are a blur in the water and send it spinning in circles. With two pairs of eyes it hunts living or dead animals. One pair sees above the surface, the other searches below. A whirligig beetle has an air supply under its shell that helps it float. If it is frightened, it can dive under the water and use this air to breathe.

Water striders and whirligig beetles are among the most common surface dwellers in ponds. Insects that fall in the water provide most of the food for them and other surface dwellers.

Other insects and insect larvae live in the water of ponds. Perhaps you saw some crawling on plants you inspected. They also swim through the water or creep along the bottom. In a pond large enough for bigger animals you may see turtles, fish and crayfish. These water animals feed at all levels from the surface to the bottom of the pond.

There is more food for scavenging on the bottom of the pond than anywhere else. It rains down constantly from plants and animals that die on the surface or in the water. In a pond with a good deal of plant and animal life, a thick carpet of sediment builds up on the bottom. Some animals suck this bottom ooze through a tube in their bodies and remove the food particles from it. They are called filter feeders. Filter means to remove solids from a liquid.

Did you find any clams in the bottom of your pond? Look carefully in the mud. There may be some clams so tiny you can hold a dozen in the palm of your hand. Clams are filter feeders. They move through the sediment on a muscular foot that stretches out and pulls the clam after it. At the end of the clam opposite the foot are the entrance and exit opening of the siphon (the tube through which the mud is sucked). If you put a clam in pond water that is not muddy, you can see the two openings. The larger one is the entrance. You may need a magnifying glass to see them on small clams.

Other animals seek food on the bottom. Worms, insects, and snails burrow down into the mud or live on top of it. Turtles capture live fish and other animals and eat those that are dead. Catfish feel around over the bottom with sensitive barbels that hang like whiskers from their chins.

Some of the scavengers and where you can find them in a pond: 1. Water strider. 2. Whirligig beetle. 3. Gnat larva hanging from bottom of surface film where he feeds on decaying material. 4. Snails. 5. Limpet, a type of snail with a tent-shaped shell. 6. Midge larva. Larva of a small fly. Eats living and dead plant material. 7. Backswimmer beetle eating a dead tadpole. 8. Clams. 9. Segmented worms. They are similar to earthworms. 10. Mayfly larva tunneling through mud, eating as he goes. 11. Tubifex worms with heads in mud siphoning it through their siphon system and filtering out food particles. 12. Snail traveling along bottom. 13. Caddisworms, larvae of caddisfly. They eat plant material. 14. Turtle. 15. Catfish. 16. Crayfish.

You can watch some smaller kinds of catfish
hunting food in many aquariums. Look along the
bottom for a fish bouncing along nose down to the
gravel. If he has whiskerlike barbels, he is a catfish.
There are other bottom feeders without barbels in
some aquariums. They are not catfish, but they are
scavengers.

You can also find scavengers clinging to plants
and other objects in aquariums, even to the glass
sides. They slide along holding on with sucker attachments, cleaning algae and dead materials from
the surfaces as they go. One of the most common
in fish tanks today is a kind of catfish, Plecostomus.
Their lips form sucker attachments around their
mouths. Light-colored and flattened on the bottom
side, spotted brown or gray on top, they slither
along swishing their pointed tails. If you find one
on the glass, you can see how it holds on with its
sucker lips.

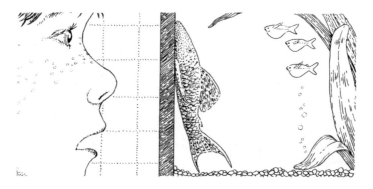

Sometimes there are snails in aquariums. You can see them hold on with a muscular foot that extends out under their shell. If you watch a snail eating as it glides along the glass side of the aquarium, you can see how it gets its food. A tongue-like part, called a radula, covered with rows of tiny teeth, rubs back and forth against the glass. That tooth-covered radula works like a file scraping off algae. Most snails in natural waters and on land have radulas and eat by filing away at dead and living plants, instead of biting and chewing.

Because it is not a natural, balanced environment, there are usually not enough scavengers in aquariums to do the whole job of keeping the tank and water clean and healthful, but they do help keep it clean, by picking up food and dead plant material that fall to the bottom.

5.

The Small Garbage Disposers

THERE ARE THOUSANDS of different kinds of insect scavengers. Over two thousand varieties of beetles eat carrion. Many others scavenge plant material.

The most famous scavenger beetles are the scarabs. These insects roll pieces of animal dung into balls. The female lays eggs in the balls. When the larvae hatch, they eat the dung and digest it more thoroughly, breaking it into smaller pieces and simpler compounds. Scarab beetles were worshipped in ancient Egypt, Greece, and Rome. One kind was considered a symbol of life and a messenger of the sun god. The ball of dung it rolled represented the earth rotating under the sun.

Another scavenger, the resurrection beetle,

symbolized life after death. The Egyptians put them in their tombs and painted their pictures on coffins. They carved models of scarab and resurrection beetles in precious stones. You may have seen a scarab ring or pin.

Thousands of different species of rove beetles feed on all kinds of animal and vegetable matter. They, too, help reduce animal dung to usable plant food. One kind of rove beetle lives in ants' nests and resembles an ant. This beetle eats dead ants and cleans up the ants' home. In return the ants take care of the beetle's young as carefully as they do their own.

Insect scavengers live in all kinds of places all over the world. Some of them even come into homes. You may sometimes see ants in your kitchen. If there are just two or three, they are probably scouting for a good food supply. If they find a tiny pile of sugar or a bit of meat, you may have a steady stream of ants carrying the food back to their nest. Food they find in your kitchen is the same to them as any other dead plant or animal matter.

Cockroaches are common in warm climates. Some kinds live outside. Others prefer cracks and dark places in houses. They will eat anything, even paper and glue. Leave a cracker on the counter in your kitchen overnight. If a cockroach lives nearby, you'll likely find his chewing marks on the cracker in the morning.

Termites are important scavengers in nature. Trees and branches fall in the forests and jungles. They need to be returned to the soil as plant food. Decomposers can do this more easily with the help of scavengers who can digest wood. Most animals

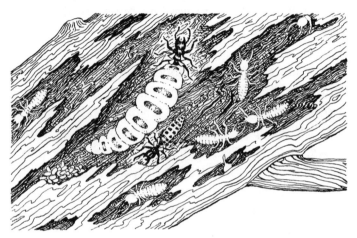

cannot, because they cannot digest cellulose, the material that makes wood strong and tough. A termite can handle cellulose, though, because it has helpers. These helpers are one-celled animals, called protozoa, that live in its digestive system. They change cellulose into a form the termite can digest. Some cockroaches also have protozoa that live inside them and help them digest wood.

Find a decaying log or piece of wood in the woods or fields. Open it up and see how many kinds of small animals you can dig from its insides. You may uncover ants, pillbugs, grubs, beetles, worms, and many others. If you cannot go into the woods or fields, look for old boards, cloth, paper, or piles of leaves that have been lying on the ground for a long time. Under them you are bound to find some small scavengers.

After the chewing and digesting of these scavengers has softened the wood, decomposers become more active. Are mushrooms, molds, or other fungi growing on your log? Even if you do not find them they are probably there. The part of fungi we usually see, such as mushrooms, is the fruit of the plant. The main part is hundreds of little threads that tunnel through the wood like tiny roots. As they tunnel they dissolve the wood. They feed on it and insect

dung. Bacteria are also busy decomposing tiny wood pieces and dung. These fungi and bacteria gradually change wood into chemical compounds plants use for food.

As more and more wood is chewed up and decomposed, the soft, damp material it becomes is a good place for small animals and decomposers to live. More and more appear, and the process speeds up. The soft material becomes a dark, crumbly, earthlike substance called humus. For plants this is the good stuff in the soil. It contains food elements they need. It is just right for holding enough water for them to use, but not so much that they drown or rot. Roots and stems grow through it easily.

If your log is soft near the surface, you may see green plants growing on it already. Ferns often grow on rotting logs.

Some bushes and trees start life on rotting logs.
A seed falls into a crack in the bark. The root of a
young tree grows into the humus inside. Years pass
as the log gradually turns into a layer of humus on
top of the soil and the tree grows larger. Its roots
grow down into the soil. Soil animals carry the humus underground and mix it with the dirt. The roots
of the new tree feed on the remains of the log.

It takes several years to decompose a tree trunk
completely. The same scavengers and decomposers

change leaves, twigs, animal dung and other debris on the ground into humus much more quickly. Soil animals mix the debris and humus with the dirt, and the soil is rebuilt for more plant growth.

Small soil animals and decomposers work side by side. The scavengers include insects, insect larvae, millipedes, centipedes, slugs, snails, and earthworms. Plant matter and dung dropped by larger animals is broken down into powder-sized pieces by these smaller scavengers.

When earthworms and millipedes tunnel by eating their way through the dirt, they mix this powdered matter with the soil. Decomposers (mostly fungi and bacteria) are found everywhere, but they are most plentiful in the soil. Mixing the powdered material with soil makes it easier for decomposers to break it down. Gardeners like to have earthworms in the soil. They sometimes even buy worms to put in their gardens. Earthworm castings (dung) are sold to use for growing plants in pots. This potting soil is rich in plant material and the animal dung the worms digested and mixed with dirt. Decomposers quickly change chemicals in the castings into food elements for green plants.

Decomposers make these changes while they are feeding themselves. Although they are not green, fungi and bacteria are plants. They absorb food through their outer walls. Since they are plants, their waste products are not dung, but chemicals they give off into the soil and air. Some of these are chemical compounds the green plants need to grow.

You can watch decomposers work at home. It's easy to grow mold on a piece of bread. Mold spores are everywhere. They grow best where it's warm and damp. Touch both sides of a small piece of bread to the floor and get a really good supply of spores on it. Put it in a jar with a drop or two of water. Screw the lid on to keep the bread from drying out. Do not put it in sunlight or on something hot. Within a week or two you will see green, yellow, or black mold growing over the bread. When the bread is completely covered, break it in pieces and see what the inside looks and feels like.

Soil animals and decomposers perform the last steps in returning nutrients to the soil. The humus they make carries plant nutrients back to the soil. Then, more plants can grow to keep the food cycle going.

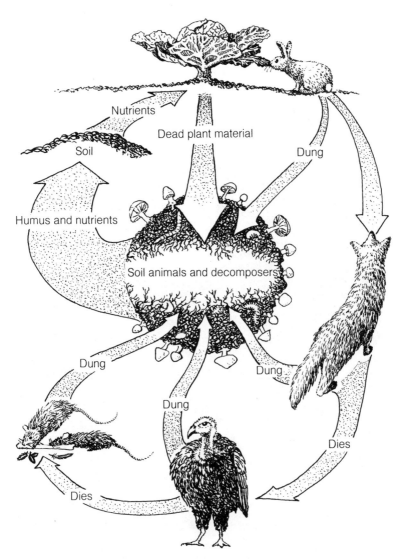

Nutrients

Soil

Dead plant material

Dung

Humus and nutrients

Soil animals and decomposers

Dung

Dung

Dung

Dies

Dies

All animals drop dung. Soil animals and decomposers change dung and other dead material into plant nutrients and humus and return them to the soil.

6.

People and Earth's Recyclers

F OR CENTURIES people believed they were masters over nature. They completely wiped out some species of plants and animals. They used plants, animals, and soil as if they had been created merely for humans to consume. They acted as if earth's cycle of life was something nature operated just to supply people with food, clothing, shelter and entertainment.

We are beginning to realize that we are a part of the food cycle just like any other animal. Some farmers and gardeners are returning plant materials to the soil. Sewage sludge from many towns is being used for fertilizer. Some of the poisons that have been killing scavengers and decomposers are no longer used. We are doing better, but we have a long way to go.

We now realize that all living things are a part

of the cycle of life. This gives us reason to respect all forms of life, even those that do things we would not.

IN LATE FALL the garden soil rests under a blanket of leaves and grass clippings. Beneath them soil animals and decomposers are working. Rotting apples lie on top of the leaves.

A flock of robins swoops down and lands. They peck hungrily at the fruit, refueling for the next leg of their flight south. They pay for their meal by leaving their droppings and opening the apples to make it easier for the small soil animals and decomposers to change them to humus. Next summer, when the gardener picks his beans and corn, he will owe some thanks to these robins.

Every time we eat anything we owe thanks to some scavengers somewhere. That thanks is also due when we enjoy the beauty of flowers, shade of a tree, coolness of grass on our bare feet, or the song of a bird.

The gardener even owes his thanks to the hundreds of slugs in his wintery garden plot. With slug bait and traps he fights all summer to keep them out of his garden, where they eat his young plants and the vegetables he plans to harvest. Now that it is winter, they are working away at the dead plant material, helping turn it into humus for his plants next spring.

Slimy, creepy-crawly, or grotesque animals we see eating dead and rotting plants and animals are not really ugly after all. They are an important part of the cycle that gives us life.

Glossary

Absorb: take in.

Ammonia: a gas made of one part nitrogen and three parts hydrogen.

Carcass: dead body of an animal.

Carrion: dead and decaying bodies of animals.

Cellulose: main part of plant fibers.

Chemical compound: two or more kinds of chemicals combined to make something different than its parts, such as hydrogen and oxygen gases combined to make water.

Decomposers: living organisms that break down wastes and dead material into simpler chemical compounds.

Droppings: dung.

Dung: animal excrement, waste materials from animals' digestive systems.

Earthworm castings: earthworms' dung.

Element: the simplest chemical piece. It cannot be broken into anything simpler by ordinary chemical actions.

Fungus (plural: fungi): nongreen plant without stems and leaves, such as mushrooms, toadstools, molds and mildews.

Herbivore: animal that eats plants.

Humus: crumbly brown or black substance that results from
  decay of plant and animal material.

Manure: animal dung put on or into the soil to fertilize it.

Nitrate: a plant nutrient containing one part nitrogen
  combined with three parts oxygen.

Nutrient: anything that serves as food for a plant or animal.

Scavenger: any animal that eats decaying animal or plant
  matter.

Sediment: matter that settles to the bottom of a liquid.

Sewage sludge: material remaining after treatment of wastes
  carried to sewage plants.

Talon: claw.

Other Books About Scavengers and Decomposers

BEHNKE, FRANCES L. *The Natural History of Termites.* Charles Scribner's Sons, 1977, New York.

COLE, JOANNA. *Cockroaches.* William Morrow & Co., 1971, New York.

DINNEEN, BETTY. *Family Howl.* Macmillan, 1981, New York. (About jackals.)

EIMERLE, SAREL. *Gulls.* Simon & Schuster, 1969, New York.

HESS, LILO. *The Amazing Earthworm.* Charles Scribner's Sons, 1979, New York.

HOPF, ALICE L. *Misunderstood Animals.* McGraw-Hill, 1973, New York.

KAVALER, LUCY. *Wonders of Fungi.* John Day, 1964, New York.

MILNE, LORUS J. AND MARGERY. *Nature's Clean-up Crew: The Burying Beetles.* Dodd, Mead & Co., 1982, New York.

PRINGLE, LAURENCE. *Listen to the Crows.* Harper & Row, 1976, New York.

SCHALLER, GEORGE AND KAY. *Wonders of Lions.* Dodd, Mead & Co., 1982, New York.

SCHREIBER, ELIZABETH ANN AND RALPH W. *Wonders of Sea Gulls.* Dodd, Mead & Co., 1975, New York.

WHITE, WILLIAM. *An Earthworm is Born.* Sterling Publishing Co., 1975, New York.

Index